AMERICÓN
NICO VELA PAGE

AMERICÓN
NICO VELA PAGE

WENDY'S SUBWAY

CONTENTS

×

A NEW PATCH OF SAND
[New Mexico, USA]
7

Lamy Station Cycle
Smoke Psalm
23

Greenthread
Interlude
57

Leave the Porch
Alone in Its Vision
87

PANAMERICANA
[Darién Gap, Abya Yala]
95

AMERICÓN/CHILESBIAN
[Santiago, Chile]
117

Huerto (Fragmentos)
133

Customs Declaration
147

Notes & Sources
175

Acknowledgments
185

For all my grandparents: Tata Pato, Tita, Ia, Bita, Tata Bill and Claudia, and my great-grandmother Priscilla.

*I am your ancestor. You know next-to-nothing
about me.*

　—C.D. Wright, "Our Dust"

*En las tardes de invierno
cuando un sol equivocado busca a tientas
los aromas de primaveras perdidas,
va mi padre en su Dodge 30
por los caminos ripiados de la Frontera
hacia aldeas que parecen guijarros o perdices echadas.*

　—Jorge Teillier, "Retrato de
　mi padre, militante comunista"

A NEW PATCH OF SAND

Gōzō commits his body to the place itself. He is physically there like an antenna scanning for place-memory and sensitive as well to his own influence and interaction ... To commit your body to a place is to begin inhabiting the world. Gōzō's radical gambit is to offer himself to a landscape in complete openness and without any preconceived goal. His whole body becomes a listening.

> — Yoshimasu Gōzō,
> "gozoCiné interview"
> by Forrest Gander

Lay me

                        out

            a way

entre   enter   y

Porch is a place
on the edge — of out
side — near the house
touching but between
door and threshold — to high
desert (so we call this semiarid
shrubland — piñon —
junipers and shabby cacti).
Even the ecosystem
indecisive and between. Porch

a way to neither here
nor there. Porch —
doesn't much care
about shelter. Won't
leave you — all alone
either — you can be less
or more home
or away
on porch.
Not a very busy
place. Porch is an inside

out beside the house:
the huerto — cold
frame for basil, oregano,
tomates, chiles — kitchen
garden beside the brick

porch beside the house
and half under the roof
going long
beyond the walls. I want

the way porch is between.

I came across a tree — so
    dry it creaked in
        wind, and creek bed

carried the dryness down
    where water was —
        deaf as drought can be.

        Pebble pebble murmured
            the gully down all
                the way — I slipped

    down tumble
        into a thicket
            of willows: venomous

    growth overtaking bank
        and fence buried
            in sand, my limbs

    wrapped in their branches
        barbed — swallowing breath
            into thick shade. At wash

bottom the river, beaver-
      pooled kneecap-high
           removed boots, socks,

rolled pant legs — so hoisted
      I dragged through —
           praying leeches

                    wouldn't want me
                    like they did

                    when we three
                    played, sisters
                    in the sulfur

                    mud.
                    Ran back
                    to the house

from tree, creek, thicket,
teeth buried
in our ankles.

                    ✕

                    Open the summer
place of cleft sand. Here, sky sits at tables so wide you
forget cliffs, at the edge, yellow, valleys, hippie, towns,
for, get the de, so,   late,   trailer   parks

                            La acequia:
     "both a traditional irrigation ditch and a politi-
cal subdivision of the State of New Mexico"
                              the basic unit of life

Parciantes   acequia members: property owners
                        along a ditch with water rights
Mayordomo   acequia manager: elected
                      to coordinate, supervise, allot
Commissioners   elected, usually three:
                         chair, secretary, treasurer
Ditch Bitch   self-appointed[1]
           each have their roles as custodians.
They flood and maintain, meet once a year to clean
and dispute and distribute. Water measured in
time. The narrow flow, its history and its people, a
collective by dint of   land   along   a ditch—

---

1. "Disruptive, uncooperative, need to contest suggestions
just as the rest of the group reaches consensus, egotistic,
tries to find fault with others' ideas, defensive to an extreme,
over-impressed with own self-righteous 'facts,' closed-minded,
picayune, spoiled brat, doesn't work well with others. I could
go on... Do you know someone like that?"
 —Tata, on-and-off mayordomo for twenty years

de la Cueva: "Remember the 8' tall cross on the west side of 111 not a mile below our house. That marks the Cemetery of the dismantled town of La Cueva. Almost straight up from the caves on the far side of the river. La Cueva was built in 1825, ten or so years before Spain turned loose of Mexico's independence. It was the first defensive settlement up from Ojo Caliente whose ditch has a Priority Date of 1795."

The language is sing-song on the first syllable and round, round on the vowels and bien drawn out, each word's tail end dragged a mile on the back of the trocka before it   hits, after the

Country is cleft, no ves? New Mexico: arrive past the small profit springs of Ojo Caliente to the painted sign that announces "PIGS": junction with alliterative little route 111— a left and growing slower in threat of flooding and falling rocks   swoop   down   that   slim   road

The long cement wall before town. Built after bombing. Behind, lives my grandfather: Tata. I have always called him in Spanglish though he is gringo— enough Spanish to get by. I call his second wife grandmother as well. Don't see the need to draw blood   lines

           La Madera. The Wood,
census-designated and so-called for mills, once.
Told a train down the ravine hauled la madera.
No trace left. Industry less certain than the wood
today. There's a rich woman from New York "been
here thirty years"; my grandfolks say they've only
seen her fifteen. She's hiring from the city, moving
people into town and then ousting them in a year
or two. She's buying up land for fields she won't
depend on and unending constructions where
she won't live. Where the town potter's shining
pots fill with dust and spiders instead of bubbling
beans and blue corn. "Adoption costs," he was
known to have said

                    I'm not from here

either. Mami,[2] Dadio,[3] two sisters and I drove or rode the train out from Los Angeles, twenty hours or so, stripping off city to roads getting high and wide, wide,
>   wide—

Buscando ahora un signo in water or clay, piñon o wild
>   sage ¿that this is mine to tell?

×

---

2. Always call her in our mother tongue.
3. Daddy-O, as my sisters and I said, became Tío Dadio in Southern cousins' mouths.

Not even trees falling
        from fruit can pick
my body off this ground
        that shatters — pulls
into itself too quick
        my thick, my feign —

a thought — on the blue
        blanket I have lain
to catch the peaches,
        peaches — peaches' weight.
Branches reproach me for
        the fruit that makes

them bow and split,
        tumble — ripe fissures:
my chest, the drought, both
        stressed, they open wide
a thirst on the bruised
        blanket — bundled now

and overfull
        with curves (my body's want).
Now sink — now rise,
        like yeast — now suck — the sweet
of slices dried —
        abundance to contain

   and save for slimmer
      days of slimmer loves.
We — fit for
     falling
       bursting
       ✕   becoming.

LAMY STATION CYCLE

SMOKE PSALM

Maybe I wake
up earlier, every muscle stream
in warmth of first simple rise
in weeks. Strands of Lamy
Station, New Mexico, still pull

from bed: Lamy my end
of the once *Santa Fe Railway*

From LA, never riding
past "No Checked
Baggage"   one room
waiting   beside overgrown
field former site of grand
El   Ortiz   Hotel

and the stilled-train-car
diner, and   still   the manual Time
Table for the Southwest Chief.

February 26, 2018 at 7:18 am, a text mess
age from my middle sister: the potter Felipe Ortega of La Madera, New Mexico

"died this weekend. :(

:("

(sister who made the prized vessel when we apprent,iced that summer,
all smoothly "glit,ters
like g,old." And she
relinqui,shed it un
caring — I held my miss
shapen pot tight till it cracked). Then Tata's "fat fingers" reply

on my mourning phone:

"@   @U betcha. & we are
wide awake. Need to think
up and write a eulogy
                         "

"Friday night or "Saturday morning. And
@   @wish I knew how to   "

On either side

      the tracks   open, land
scape far t,wi s ting
        into gullies and cañones
            the, distance, between

          "   the specific clay that I will speak about
found eroding from rich mica schist deposits in the Sangre
de Cristos and San Juan Mountains of northern   "

Sm,all trees
Scrib,bled brush
Low cact,us   giving
                         each other space

"Telltale mark that announces the presence

                                           abundance of quartz and feldspar"

          "Mica in the clay body acts as a temper and also gives
                                           the clay body"

(EeeeuuUU and the falling wooden fence, where smaller legs s(w)ung in the photo streaming from desk/top/back/ground/wall/paper/under/sky while we waited (&.........*awake*) the tra,in: 2008 memory.

Lamy my station –
translate me

"Preparing and caring for your vessel"
"Turn the eye to medium hIgh"
"add several tablespoons of an,I,mal

        el humo por un himno y

   lay me in this
   micaceous station.

fat" longing for field
fingers clay caked:
ash — ask

This weekend Don Felipe, Jicarilla Apache, Penitente Brother, New Mexican, mixed
red   s,t,a,r,s   in
to pot s and himself into horno
smoke.   Back to summer s pent walking
                  with purple   desert clouds

        to Owl Peak. We three kids
        pUSHed clay into swelling cheeks

"hand does not dance
            around the pot   "

lay wet snake upon snake:
        Felipe
        "fastest
        coiler
        in the
        west "

                                    & we are

            wide awake

                        smelling Tata's tobacco
                        jacket deep in my nose

"I urge you to place your right thumb straight smack in the middle"

Coil and   scrape
from within the vessel
begin to shape
empty beauty: "you can have
         an unclear image
             in your mind"

6. Letting the Pot Become Leather Hard

"   At last, twilight approaches, the sun, slowly
sinks. That, earth, step, rhythm, one foot, plant, the roots, are thrown all over,
the setting sun, sinks, watching, the sky roots,we drive, to Lamy Station, on
the Santa Fe Railroad.

                                                               "
                              —Yoshimasu Gōzō, trans. Richard Arno,
                              "Lamy Station"

Far from La Madera
just days after the potter
passes I read Gōzō:

Japanese poet at my
little railroad. How
did we end up

    all together? In Lamy Station
    Felipe Ortega awaits
    firing coils of a bean pot away

AY   Ay   ay   X

A NEW PATCH OF SAND

Sulfur soaking we watch
mountain disappear/in
to the sky   /losing to
the rubbing of cricket/stream
running back to

          a dirty spring.   *No*:

    algae blooms   silt/swirls

  can't mar   this bubbling

up from   soil itself.

Yet clouds   curdle
blue/black the mountain-
top — we watch it
disappear/in — lightning!
Calcifying   eyes/
hear a concert of kai-oats   :
                co / yo / tes

   sí, coyotes come play — shrieking
   laughter at our marrow/sinking —

                   soaking night across
                         ridge they run
nuestros cuerpos empapados
                                our soggy/bodies

    a way to disappear/in

             a dirty spring.   *Know*:

                ownership   New

                    Yorker   ex-husband's

Eastern European?   oil riches

      can't   slick

        the little   eye,

           called   Statue

   Spring (on   the

           map). *No*:   to us, el

               ojito   crying

in   the sand

     so we can   soak

          our   bones.

              ✕

Stumbling upon boyhood's
bones bleached blancos por

    el sol, searching for
    dryness so round
    it meets itself

        again, I kneel to love
        these harsh plants.
        Mesquite, with spikes

            of flowers, catches
            what comes in the flash
            floods of broken
            vacuums, old Christmas

                decorations,
                tires so wide
                you could
                sleep in,
                deep in
                the sand

        of wash walls. Look: down
        en este cañón hay pequeñas
        plantas amarillas, brighter

    stalks than flowers
    justo después de la lluvia
    que las levanta

with tiny drops
as the sun
drips low:

empties the arroyo, the boy-o
I was, into un tallo liviano, árido-redondo,
and brighter yellow now, my shape
shifting, a ravine after rains.

In mid of rye
question stalks
grandmother enters the field
of direction:
stream back up hill
soft clusters too
bursting and Tata
wades away

Rather I
leave my attempt
at him
on the bank
slip into the rush
soft and growing

Little tits, cactus
nips pink prickling out
lay me (crickets
rubbing around
riverbed) here
touch   me
amorphous   almost   amphibian
    ambivalent   erogenous

On a sun-soaked stone
break the stream:
in two, between,
hips, thighs, my

Touch, the planes, all
my surfaces: my southfaces   mi sur

      cara,   mi cara sur,

 please surca   my surfaces: plow

     soar   through   sí

surca   por   mi sur

      face mi sur   sex o

 mi cara azul   su sur face   of

    blue   susúrrame   súrcame score

      mi sur azul   sur cleave

  sur sail   surca: my South   mouth,

plow me   sur cara

✕

To the porch, where grandma puts holey old sheets up, diffusing morning sunlight into something pleasant. Keep the house cool. Keep the radio on all day with the news, most times, or the *Raíces* music program I like, sometimes, and very very sometimes, the Navajo airwaves to listen to the rhythm and a different sort of weather.

Chickens try to get up on the lumpy outside couch, Tata scoops some of their shit off the bricks, throws it at them. Lets the dog bark a bit, but not enough to get real excited— he'll chase.

There are piles of boxes and tools and knick-knacks and hand cream and dry things and treasure things on the table that wraps around the house. This cluttered threshold between inside and out.

There is Tata's chair. There is my grandmother's spoken-for, sunken-in spot on the couch right next to the chair. There is the rest of the couch for us and the dog and his hair. The poem I want to write. Resting there.

That couch means looking east, means the little mountain and across the fields. Straight ahead means a peach tree, a big bush, and three hummingbird feeders. Keep an eye on them and don't let them get empty or the hummingbirds will come humming to you and feint pecks at your face— give them the sugar water.

Trickling down from the right side of the house is the ditch. On our day to get water, the long metal sprinklers will be going in the fields and we will wet feet and float sticks and paper boats down the little stream, we will run beside to see if they make it over the drop after the footbridge and kneel to nudge them out of the willow roots that entangle from the bank. We will watch them rush into the shining corrugated maw of the culvert and look away when the steel streaming into our eyes begins to swim. Turn and run back up to the house to tell of all we did and saw and learned along la acequia hoy.

Between the ditch and the peach, a stand of milkweed for the butterflies.

The porch is half-covered by the roof of the house overshooting and putting beams down into the brick. If it's raining, we watch the tank fill and the water take the place of the old holey sheets rushing off the roof. In warmth we sit further out and look up from cigarettes. The changing sky. White plastic chairs glow in dusk and gossip over heavy glasses of boxed wine while the desert curls around.

Grandma gave
a linen shirt to work
the fields: flax keeps

cool and doesn't
smell (too bad at
end of day, usually)

Me quedaba
grande, cuadrillé
azul falling

loose off mis
hombros y me sentí
como Mami

and I loved
that shirt — felt
me in a femin

in way, in a plaid
lin en way y el li
no masculine ni fe me ni
no ni mas fem me
in linen ni masc en li
no   ni

masculinen

nor

femelino

✕

GREENTHREAD INTERLUDE

flowering ridge
  the second one back
    from the lighthouse

Who saved it?—
  Women
    of good wild stock

   —Lorine Niedecker,
   "Wintergreen Ridge"

Garlic to pull
   late July
      To pile

on the long porch
   table —
      brush   careful

don't rub off
   pearl-thin skin
      Measure between

two rusty nails
   Bundle tie
      hang to dry

Early August
    mow the rye
        Fixing soil I learn:

farming at core
    Vetch tangles
        among the still-soft

tumbleweed (it grows
    before it tumbles
        you know) and spider

tendrils of stickers
    to pull up
        from blade-center

Red metal and
   chest-tall wheels
      crushing and

behind
   blades spin nitrogen
      stalks into soil

Avoid the
   clusters of
      curly-haired

rayless yellow
   "thread-like slender
      leaves"   families

of Aster
   stopping my
      diesel advance

Through the
   child-high
      translucence

of rye —
   hardy cover
      slashed down

save where
   flowers halt
      my tractor

cold   From
   side-hanging
      metal basket

grab scissors
   climb down
      and kneeling find

the threads —
   "when flowers
      open (summer

and fall) and
   cut about three
      inches

from" the sand
   boots sink into
      gathering

"Before tea
   or coffee...
      New Mexico cota

was widely used
   as a beverage"
      Lining high-

ways over the pass
   atop the mesa
      buttery yellow little

shocks along
   hot tar
      but don't stop

for the exhaust-
   soaked stalks
      My armfuls

between the rye
   sufficient
      for winter

Days end shuttling back
   and forth across
      the warp of fields

gopher-pocked
   close-cropped
      the weft complete

a long loop:
   back to shed
      chicken coop

footbridge
   the house
      night-cooled

and sun-
   shuttered for
      sitting out

midday: "bending
   a handful
      of cota back

and forth, and
   then tying
      the bundle with another

stalk of cota
   to hold it
      in place"

then lay
   in a dry
      basket

As tea medicine
   stomach kidneys
      and to purify

blood as when
   dyeing with such
      threads and flowers

"the rust
   color can
      be controlled"

the yellow
   alone "a
      treasured source

×

A NEW PATCH
OF SAND

brick   wicker
warped   wood
beam   nail
log   pile
cast   iron
burlap   denim
cotton   line
screen   door

couch   chair
bench   table
coffee   mug
Abiquiu   News
Río Grande   Sun
New   Yorker
canvas   print
fountain   hammock

dog   chicken
humming   bird
wasp   nest
beaver   skull
cow   bell
fly   swatter

brush   broom
scissors   shears
gardening   gloves
straw   hat
shovel   rake
trowel   screwdriver
compass   thermometer

rain   water
barrel   bucket
basket   sack
bundle   rafter
wire   twine

laundry   pile
clothes   pin
stove   grill
horno   candle
citronella   DEET
spray   sunscreen
beeswax   balm
piñon   salve

wine   glass
radio   ashtray
porch   light

✕

elk moans
summon us to
a time before morning:
stalk-crushing moans,
river-crossing moans,
bark-stripping moans,
low-hanging

moans, we wrap tighter
around, shine lights
out to catch pairs
of eyes: night stalkers
of fields and foothills.
They wisp across furrows
fog-like, near impressions
bounding from retina-
center to forest-
edge, from our haunting
back to bed.

then cricket blue
takes over and sweeps.
Cricket blue sits heavy
on couch, wicker creaking,
pretends not to notice
the flies. Cricket blue
surprises me in the willows
so I almost step back, slip,
fall and crack the ice, set
the river tumbling. Cricket
blue won't let the grass
rest. Cricket blue insinuates itself
                        into the house, cricket
                        blue beneath the covers,
                        cricket blue spoiling bags
                        of rye in the rafters,
                        cricket blue showering
                        all the water in the well.
                        Cricket blue sucks
                        rattler poison from dog's
                        shank, spits it out
                        in my bowl.

apricots crab apples
grapes peaches pears
would climb,
   gather them
        but for   ripping

dirtying pants
when did that
               my first
                   thought?

become	distance
from soil,	skin
from worms	once
burrowed my	softness
then was not	meaning
choice but	tunnel
waterway	arch

        why dress to make
        me different only to
        worry so the clothes
        worry

sharp	bark
stain	leaves
sticky	sap

                    and
                  cringe
               from slime
            in the beaver
         dam I should clear
    for us to water, instead

     I let the backhoe
              rip the river
                 out its mud

        ✕

fire in the iron stove

the screen door shut quick behind

the crab apple trees withering

the round rug, woodchip sprinkled

the rusted toy trucks beneath the cottonwood
    (stands high over the house; once a man
    passing through town who specialized in
    cataloging trees "and their stories" heard
    of our cottonwood and came to photo-
    graph it. "Among other cameras one of his
    is an infrared," Tata said)

the windows so high up with the long, long
    drawstrings

the Middle Kingdom
        (sisters' tangled tree fort, stickers in
        your socks)

the hummingbird feeders refilled three times daily

the alcove for a woman grandmother carved
        (illuminated altar to wooden curves)

the clawfoot bathtub in the woods by the river

the blue toilet

the photos from the '90s pinned to the
    bookshelf, two melded in memory
            (Mami in a big red coat and stripy scarf,
            Dadio beneath his dark brown leather
            cowboy hat. Bolts of baby-white hair
            escape from a tiny knit beanie; strapped
            to my father's chest. Cheeks overflowing
            the folds. Not that my father has folds:
            clothes float around his then-slender
            length. A big old dog stands nearby, a dog
            whose name I should— Chester? They
            look prepared. A hike or a road trip, per-
            haps. Faces simply. Open. See. The sky.
            About to rain, the whole scene washed
            a little blue. A young Chilean, a younger
            gringo. This child in the middle)

the shallow dog bed, dogless

the drawer with twin metal tubs for sugar
    and flour built into the kitchen cabinet
        (one day the sourdough in the bowl by the
        stove grew and grew over and out and onto
        the counter, dough spreading thick across
        the kitchen, and we wondered what was so
        ripe in the air— the plum wine fermenting
        in the mudroom off-gassing? pollen? the pi-
        lot light acting up? the extra heat of visitors
        in the house?)

the winter light slipping in under
        (as sun turns hotter, higher in the sky,
        eaves' angle cuts the summer shine and
        keeps the night cool in)

LEAVE THE PORCH ALONE IN ITS VISION

I came across a tree — so
dry it creaked in
the wind, and the creek carried
its dryness down to
the water —
               was deaf. Watch

the mountain disappear in
to the sky — head might be up
there, drowning
in the rubbing
of crickets, the stream running
back to a dirty spring.

Not even the trees — falling
from fruit can pick
my body off this ground
that shatters — pulls
me into itself too
quickly.

               I am being a little lonely
        even though my grandma tells me not to.

The white plastic
chairs glow in dusk and gossip
over grandparents' boxed
wine. The desert

curls around us, swallows
into a ball of *was.*

All these songs
end before I'm
ready, somehow right
when I want them
to leave me with
rustling, gurgling
or flickering automatic lights
that won't
silence for
  — coyote yips — elk moans — cricket blue —

Come morning, leaves'
shrill rub: I would
scale them
for sweet
if not for ripping,
dirtying pants   —   wonder
when was that my first   thought?

How I cringed from
the slime in the beaver
dam I should clear
for us to drink but instead
let the fucking backhoe

                                      rip the river
                                      out of its mud.

                              I am gentle and soft.
                                Like cottonwood.
                                  With roots up
  turned in the water where I stand —
  on light bark — tumble into beaver
  pond — swamp us all. Pond's taken ev-
  ery trace of bridge, trace of my mud-
  dy knees and band-aid-arms. Stinks
  like me — this constancy of bareness
                belly chest and ankles
                     for the world: testament
                     challenge   or proof

of   Weaving
a body between —

PANAMERICANA

cruzar piernas
cruzar palabras
cruzar países

My family dreams of driving
the Pan-American Highway

"And why does it remain unfinished
an imagined geography
a study in contradictions, torn between
      goodwill and self-interest,
      cooperation and control,
      pragmatism and paranoia
community forged in asphalt and concrete

a bright red line, like a hemispheric aorta

all of whom, by and large, opposed state
	control
'mental agony,' his frayed psyche buoyed
		with images of 'the shining stream of
		motor cars which one day
		would thread the jungle'
mud at least one hundred feet deep
in light of its glib conclusion that the
	current route might lead to the
	'cultural extinction' of the Cuna and
	Chocó

barely sixty miles
'If the Berlin Wall fell, why can't the
	Darien Gap'
'it acts as a land bridge where species from
		both continents intermingle'"

barely sixty
miles an imagined
geography mud at least
one hundred feet
deep community
forged in asphalt and
concrete all of whom by
and large opposed
state control if the Berlin
Wall fell why can't
the Darién
Gap a study in contradictions torn
between goodwill and self-
interest cooperation and
control pragmatism
and paranoia it acts as a land
bridge where species
from both continents
intermingle and why
does it remain
unfinished mental agony
his frayed psyche
buoyed by images
of the shining
stream of motor
cars which one day would
thread the jungle a bright red
line like a hemispheric
aorta in light of

its glib
conclusion that the current
route might lead to the cultural
extinction of the Cuna
and Chocó

A bright red
mud opposed
contradictions.

                    And why sixty miles
between goodwill
and concrete:
if at least both intermingle
mental one the hundred feet
the shining stream
agony line it
thread the current
cultural extinction
its glib conclusion
might lead to a hemispheric aorta.

Psyche from deep
in that species bridge.

                    All of whom, by
self-pragmatism remain
forged in the Darién Gap,
fell as a land
buoyed by one
day motor cars
and large acts,
imagined geography.

Study torn cooperation
and control in asphalt,
like the Berlin Wall,
a jungle which would light
continents: barely,
community paranoia
can't interest his frayed
images of state control.

                                                Of the Cuna
                                                and Chocó.

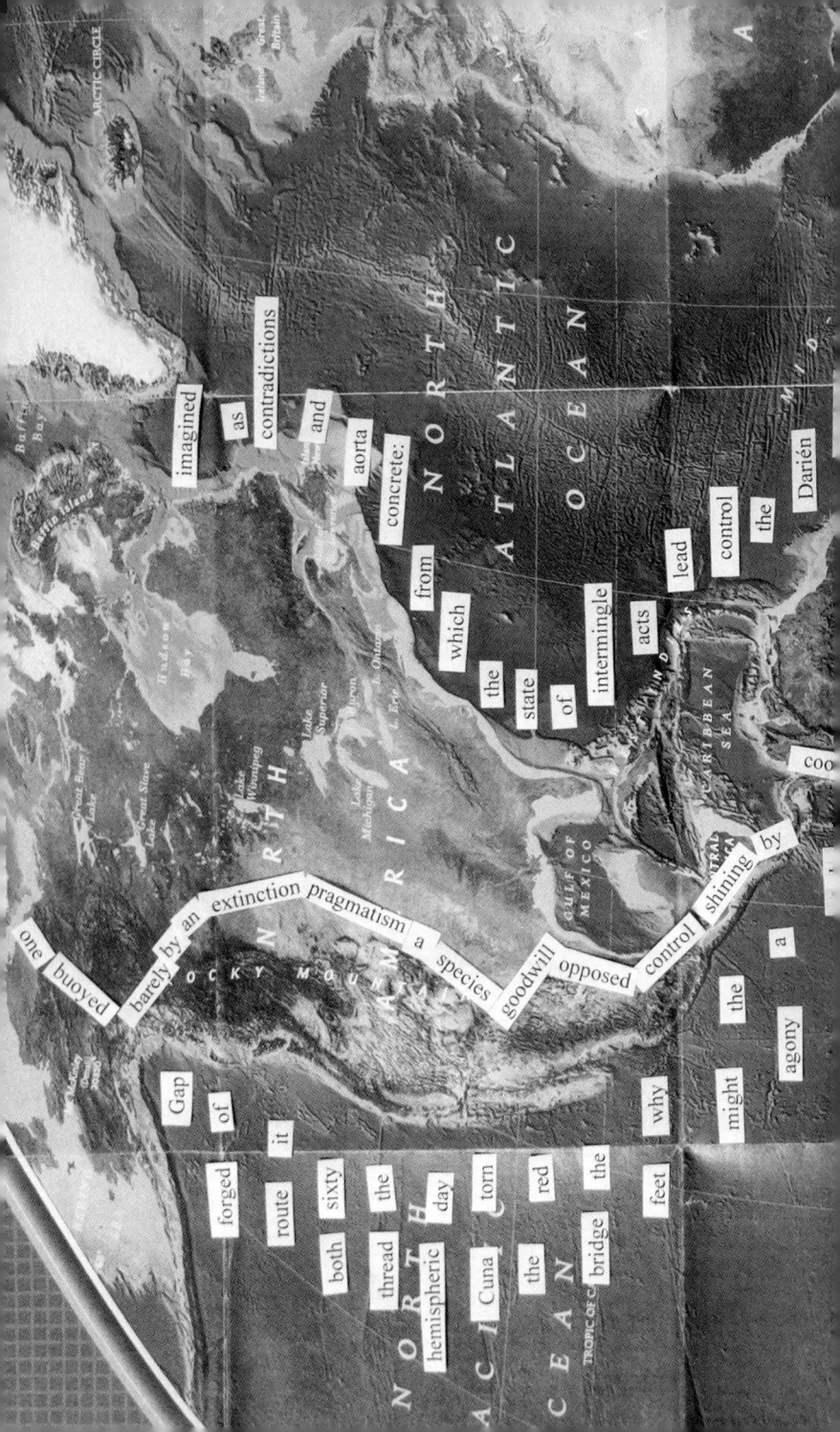

imagined as contradictions and aorta concrete: from which the state of intermingle acts lead control the Darién

one buoyed barely by an extinction pragmatism a species goodwill opposed control shining by the a agony

Gap of it why might

forged route both sixty the torn day red feet
thread hemispheric Cuna the bridge the

land
mental
community and
cars deep
between
all
fell a
current
of asphalt
a
mud that
Chocó bright
Berlin its paranoia in whom can't
continents: geography
would one and self- interest to light in like of
conclusion line motor glib and miles where stream and
least
Wall

América en su turbio centro se resiste
a tu mirada: continente sobre-
metaforizado como cuerpo
y a que le declares:
un sexo u otro;
pasto y maleza,
fango y pantano,
selva y montaña
ahí donde te gustaría
No, América no es ni
madre ni padre sino masa
de tierra   simplemente, no
                                      metá

America at murky center resists your
gazing at: continent over-
metaphorized as body
and pronouncing it:
one sex or another;
grass and brush,
slime and marsh,
jungle and mountain
there where you'd like to
No, America is neither
mother nor father but land
mass   merely, not
for

But imagine setting out from Tierra del Fuego on a trans
    study in contra
    crossing Amé
    the body of the cont
    highway scars post-op
    passing through b
    between gend   ers   dictions:

                                        rica

                              in ent

                        er: a ti on

                                orders

                                          to you   does my conti
                                                       nent:
                                                        cunt
                                                          in

                      p a n a m e r i c a n a

                                                                                       dress
                               nor te
                               nor   country   ✗

                                                             cross continent
              me
                          ent re enter
                          cunt in entry
                          entre enter y

         sur
tran s it
       ando

                                                    lay my
                                                a bright
                                                red   line
                                            across   eye
                                                    liner

                        across sur face

                                    lid: red
                                                dad y
                        acros s ur face

                                    mi mud splotched skin
                                        mud ando

                    mi suave
                bundo
            las manchas de Mami
    Dadio vaga

self

                                                                                    between water

                                                                          ass   be comes

                                                                 gap

                                                        and   gr

                                                mud mi

                        pant ano

              able
      cruz
      selva
      se vuelve

falda in

donde

```
                                                face
                                                u line
                                                red

                                         shining stream
                                         thread the jungle




                         aorta abierta




                                              stitch mi postoperación




         masc
         a r a




sur
ca
ra
```

selvulva

where amé

mi rica my gap

mi carretera my collapse

mi sueño de crossing me

panamerican

X

AMERICÓN

Hyphens between
lay me   a life. In there
and back aga in s a way —

       – Chilean – American –
        – trans – femme –
        – non – binary –

entre aquí and allá. Reject attempts to defi
ne me defi
le me defi
re me defy
    bounds
    as between the fall
    of q en línea
    recta, círculo nacido,
    to tilde y l y l y
    tilde. Caída
    de la q convirtiéndose
    en dip en la u — so, silent
    slipping. High ll —
    vectores, abstracciones
    de dirección and length,
    twist like language —
    let hyphens lie

A aa a aya ay ya a su comienzo su curl
like coming home and looping
away, my flight patterns en
círculo encircling mis aquís
y my allá. í
        is me

                          leap

   slowly

        from here to there.

See the ´ saltando:
aquí, allá, una pequeña
parábola.   ping!

Si solo fuera
tilde   jumping
again from the a, resorte
al próximo   ahí
donde me encuentro
yo, entre enter y exit
    exist o

A transitivity to
nation, porous
like my boys

try to hold my
body, *he* me
I slip! cross
again. What home am I

holding anyway, going on
about cute tops
and leggings, on the radio
legs *crossed the Great Plains, rushing
into Wisconsin when they opened
that border   settlers*, I think
What a hell (como dice Mami):

thieves. Might steal
my testicles tuck
them deep   a hole

for another   to grow.
There's a rewrite:
the poem greets (on the way
out). Because what a hell

is a home anyway. We'll have
a new declaration
of indeference, sodomy
and switches, us

bitches the new queens. The land that was

open arms,   crumbling   the

        unsteady   house

                    sinking.

×

Evacuate: take   and slip
out   create
of innards and vessels: pile

       the sidewalk with / rubble: beams
           cable   nails   long

memory of last night:

      Desire   must it always?
      transgress   yet   stay
      in the palm   of the mouth, all

most palatable. Still

                          breaking
           brittle
stained
nails filing out
in rows from shaking: houses
where meaning flees

As for the glitter factory:
                       the biggest

   market:

my hands —

                              palms secreting
                             shine manufacture
                          dust into   unwanting

pursuit: an   intimation

      so defined:
         biology,   constructed,   in,
         opposition,   and,   in,
         deed,   shaped,   by,

           a squeeze
on the surface: causing tremors, forcing

mountains out of two:
         diligence overdue.   Catching,
         anoche   on fresh
         skin and   shoulds.

                              Transgression
                     that's in the hand, the slide of

                         binary
                         masses
                         tectonic
                       giving rise
                      to cordillera
                     a range between

sly plays: I
      know yours
           and still.

              intim / id / ation

              trans / ag / gression

              pushing / slipping, we run,

              out of our / houses at the groaning

              pace of beams / for collapse and gape / for

              lips pursed like tectonic / blades

              for a mountainous kiss

              for / love / s

              split

              ✕

From away, Santiago a veces aparece
in my head — streets as
dreams stretch out
from my feet, las calles
vacías: foggy, dark, often
or tree-shrouded; familiar
but never my street,
not the daily streets I wore
down under school-
bound bike tires.
Rather, the occasional

exploratory pasaje, the empty
avenida in a neighboring
neighborhood, my nearby
streets where I threaded
wheels between white:
— —
stitching entre los autos
agresivos, luchando
por mi espacio: donde vereda
and asphalt meet (mi gutter):

                the same tar outside
                my window here, in
                Providence — como Providencia,
a Santiago barrio — se ríen mis amigues
entre pantallazos — ahora las cletas des
        cansando. How do these cities all
        feel so same? So car-hard and against
        trees and people. Esta falta:
        de imaginación we call colonialism.
        Santiago, Providence, Los Angeles
        such divine
                        cities have made we
— — — — — — — —~~anything but holy.~~— — — —
                        Built — mercilessly.

Yet I love these streets, their rip
and glaring   my friends
and I can hardly cross.

✕

Arrested in the brutal
scroll of beatings, chanting, broken
eyes, repeating, in all these years

away, the bougainvillea has expanded
across the whole sky of the garden, almost
reaching the curly-haired jasmine —
unfolding hopeful from its clinging
to the wall — and the full apricot
tree, three kissing so only a skinny sliver
of evening sun rests

on my knees, sliver
of stomach, warmed
cheeks full of melisa
and lemon peel and cedrón tea: tisane,
to be precise: agüita,
we call it: little water,
herb tea: a little
water to sip: come sit

with me, sharing that too, good
feeling, at core, como agüita
wandering a glowing
city with our beautiful
friends while little visions
around us, all around us

fall, days shrinking somewhere deep
inside where not even slivers
of shrapnel can slip: not even tear
gas can seep: where you reach—
through me — grasp the future we
want to see — so badly I could
cry: we cry sounding like grain

HUERTO
(FRAGMENTOS)

What a strange and ghoulish intimacy they had with the young people they tortured and murdered.

I saw a wall of photographs too at the Museum of Memory and Human Rights, Avenida Matucana in Santiago. I said, oh my god. I sat for some time.

> —Dionne Brand,
> "Docile Bodies,"
> *The Blue Clerk*

      el invernadero

                            su constancia
no es de aquí:
    plantas

              sin estación

　　　　　mejor será

　　　　　　　　　　　　sublimarnos
　　antes de que escampe

　　　　　　　　　　　　　trenzar
　　　　　el pasto porque la tierra
　　es muy niña　　　　no puede
　　　　　　　　sola aún

　　　　　　　marineros de vidrio.

cada pisada

                        un ojo en la tierra

          parpadea, miel

   hasta

                una sombra
                un sitio blanco
                y un riachuelo

Hay unos abuelos sin hijos.

mmmadre

las manchas
en su piel viscosa

sucede que me canso de que todo
vuelva a la dictadura
Aún así,

la puerta

                          su risa

                de arena

      la mañana

punzante

                  :   pierdes
y es la adultez. Siempre va primero
la niñez, aunque sea en el ínfimo
instante antes de la primera muerte
va primero

hierbas en el jardín
el gran cedrón detrás
de la cocina

hasta que te mudas
a un departamento
sola. con la perra

por aquí no viaja
el sonido, solo
por la madera
y el deseo

×

CUSTOMS DECLARATION

Waistline leaves
the skin
desired. How
does this
ass look? Turn
around   peek   over   practice

      presentation: high
      waists and short
      shirts; dangling
      from ears, twirls
      delicate; socks
      sneak an ankle
      to the cold; a scarf

tossed just so

you might look
and ask

the commas,,,,be,come paddle,,,strokes,,,left,,,right,,,in the body,,,,of word,s,wim,ming,a,cross,,,the page, the b,lank,,,p,age,,,,an age of,f,ew"'com,mas,,, commun,l,cate,,,a cross on the body of water,,,the waves,,,, slashes in the p,ape,r,r,are,,,p,in,points of sight, pricks,,,a milk,y,way spilt / split a cross the page,,,wh,ere,we,re,ad / we,da,re / with eyes / drop,ping ,,,,, out / our sock/et/s,,,slithe,ring,,,s,mud,ging,,,down word,s,ink sludge a,long,,slice,,m,y,mmm,e,y,e,li d,l ,running,,,the corner, down the side, over the mouth, dribbling the chin, peeling the neck, puzzling the chest, repopulating the stomach, insiding-out the liver, dragging the arms, to the penis, to hollow out a canoe, to the river, take the arms, off each side, us,ing, them, to, p,addle,,,,,a,,,cross,,,the,,,,words,,,cross,,,the,,legs,,,,cross,,,the,,,bod y,a,cross,a,stroke,a,,,cro ss,,,,,,dress

from English to lengua
to   don't ask where,
what, my accent, less, betraying,
my voice,s g,end,er's, my pas,sing curling
language to confusion on
sour lips: where my body is
from, that is, you ask

M   (madre)   Chile
F   (father)   USA

Please circle 1 (one).

think in grayscales weighing between:

    form and content
       man and woman
           theory and practice
                non and violence
        and non. Absence
      and presence, that's over

worked

in denying these dualisms   name them   frame my rejection through the very thing   I reject I   want to learn to think to write to move in a third space   before beyond beneath   where you are turned on without feeling your   self a gender   without having to conform a want for porn of non/white/queer people into separate little categories   where poems are so open you can't help but touch yourself   and there are no side effects to becoming   trans women getting hard sweet   easy   or you still fuck me so good soft   where desire can waver and I don't have to always choose don't have to be so sure   enthusiastic *yes*   so lone in my please for something   more   than two

Disbinary the Spanish with   *e o x*   I'm not convinced fits – as skirts –
fall well and makeup me eleva. *They took time too* – now
  it catches
  easiest

Disbinary finality. I'm not from here. Crossing over, yes, but settling
anywhere – aquí or allá, there o where – is not my aim. Changes
day by day, sometimes hour by hour. Such settling has been done
  to this body:
  unsettle

                            x

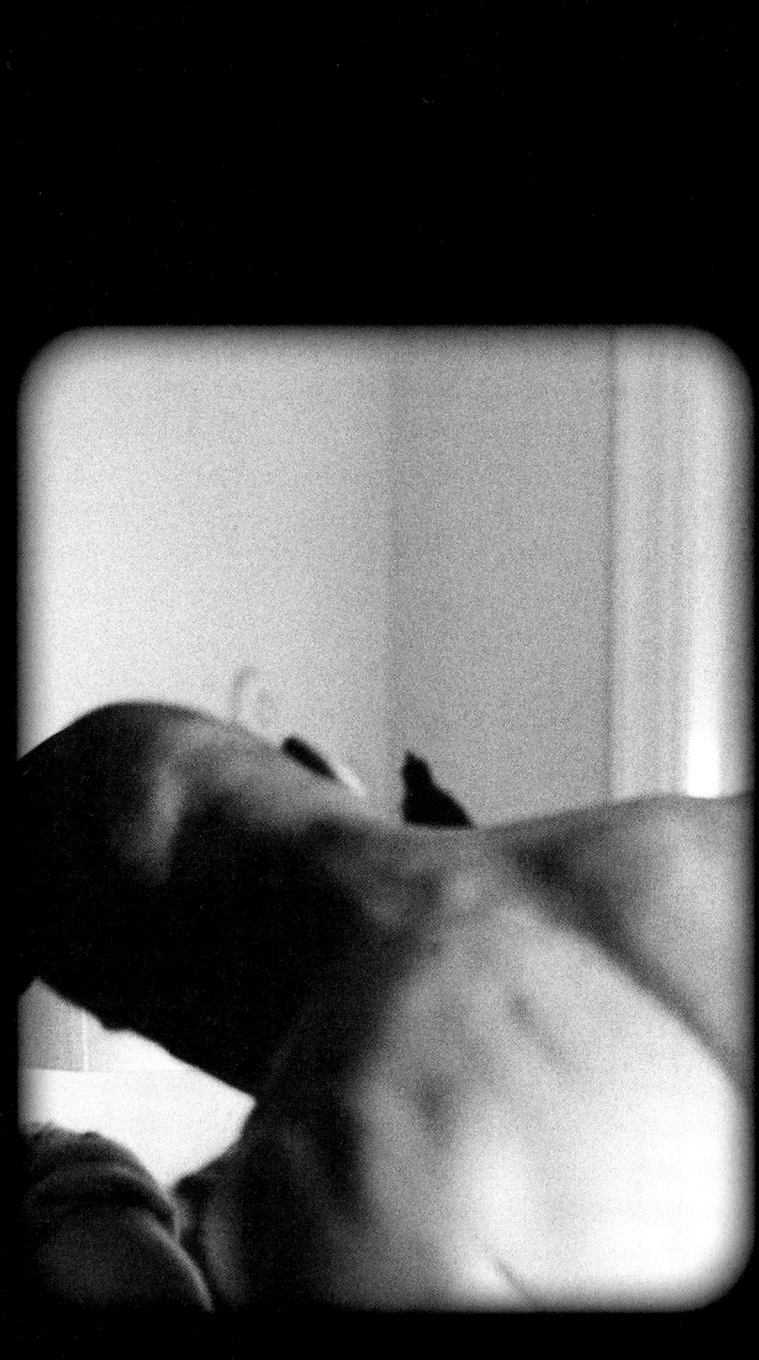

CHILESBIAN

Como querer saber secretos
  que sin ni susurrar me
    separaban de mis amigas.

Dancing at the festival
  I watched the women
    not up on stage, kissing

in the crowd, I wanted, not
  them: el amor que compartían. Volví
  con una nueva convicción:

  el amor lesbiano el más hermoso.
 Lesbian love the loveliest —
La amor lesbiana la más hermosa.

Ya no longer my dogma

           ✕

This morning you came

                                                            imagining

                yourself a pussy

you finger

        fingiendo   you   finger

                the bass
              your voice
            betrays
         say a
        scale
     of   which

                                 you have

no conception   no

you   can't   hear   your   own

        moan
        but it
        surprises:
        the depth
        like fingiendo

the base of
your tucked

your pene
tu pussy

    ×

The soil, peaty and light like crumbling confetti, seeps in all around me, filling my crevices, roots reaching out from above to curl tight around legs, arms pull me apart, almost tenderly so, I harden and the fungi tickle my tits, chest, and pussy straining against the lace of a mycorrhizal embrace, millennial memory holding me in like the earth filling my mouth warm and probing, dirt wrapping around my eyes, my back arching under decomposing, by water from deep below, cool water washed by gem, mineral, sediment-sweet water that rushes always beneath that deep water rises in my veins, wets me, to welcome the crushing weight of trees, the bears' leaping hunt, the waves making their polyrhythms on shore, calling me to move, sea's pulsing crashing in my hips loose until moon's girth lifts me, pulls me down, rocks me faster and faster along fault line I release all into the turning through tunnels at break neck speed, squeezed by worms, mole's blind paws, rabbits' darting daring, snake paths, homes tightening around my offered esophagus, my tide still filling and here my ass, my soiled, anxious heart, to plant in the world, and let myself become hole

Llegar de a poco, asking
¿why is it the spirit siempre
se demora más? Though this

        time, my body, too, in sync
        with moon cycles and seasons
        still wanted to hibernate
        when I flew across

el ecuador y de pronto, verano. Algo
traman en la cocina — se ríen
de forma malvada y libre. Sister

        and cousin — pushing
        each other into the waves,
        into stealing a fish
        from some khaki

rich old men. Swig of wine,
y *córrele córrele* — pescado
en mano. *Vegan Action*. Is the sea

        the destruction? The task is
        to translate desembocadura:
        surrender — the river opening

its mouth into the ocean, water
unmouthing into water. The destination
release? A movement? A recess

        to molecule, to recognize
        this limb as lake, brain
        as reservoir ready to join
        droplet upon droplet, slip

to stream. Precarious moments open up:
evoke constancy, presence, patience,
pleasure. Quenching as an ethic
        of giving, yes, I think I can
        expect some reciprocity.
        Express some gratitude.
        Will you, too? Learn
        to be given to?

Editing bits of me
away, not that gesture. Not that
face. My youngest sibling wonders
if they were cutting, keeping
me in place — another's grace.
But my voice mispronoun-

ces: I cut/   voice escapes
my grasp/   cut/ flickering/
fingers/ too   glamorous/   cut/
me/ flamboyant me/ hide
me/   in revision. Still learning

to be body among rocks
volcano-made, hot by hot:
sinking earth into earth,

when great gray stone sky
and pumice floats
on lake: mirror is complete.

In thick reflection grow rock
soft, broad as shore's lilting:
trans is blanket, an envelope,
space carved out where I and my
loves move elemental, unhurried
by borders. Expanding lenticular
to you —

Glacier cut   mountain:
heavy water through rock, saying
hill here river here lake
here.   So, the cutting floor:
shaping the body is the work.

Can't, but, feel,
   resonances with last
      spring, time I rolled

syllables trans,femme
   around in my
      mouth so convincing.

Can't, quite, find,
   comfort in cyclical
      questioning. More

akin to doubt, sadness
   in January or sunflowers
      too soon. In the circle

I want to lay me
   out like new
      nouns, like dripping

laundry to hang, dry, fold, she,
   hers almost wrings
      out my tongue.

      Once, in the city with a friend who is nonbinary and transmasculine, some cops lounging on their car offered — "Help crossing, ladies?": an empty intersection we had not even turned towards. But for a moment, before rage, fear, and offense, I electrified.

Ladies —
Once,

   let me be this body

walking in the street
   lights, I tell a friend
      my cycles. She finds assurance

in them: affinity with tides
   and harvests, garlic pulling
      and rye fixing: attunement

to our implicated
   nature, not doubt
      nor insincerity.

Reassure me change
   is not a lack
      of commitment, to this,

that gender, say, when
   morning is a femininity
      and by tea

time I might be masc,
   tell me, how
      do I noun?

        Return to convincing
        others. Hoping
        in what turns
        to their confusion.
        Clinging to their "miss?"
        Seconds later, apologizing
        for their apologies.

What makes my bod
   y legible? The way
      porch reveals

my surfaces, opens my
   south, my wanting
      like   cotton

wood   gentle
   and   wide.
      Tree solid.

Let me   slip
   weave   between   a
      way. Dissolving

edges: paper in water,
   pulp. Dunk the poem
      in the pond

hope for a vulva

                ✕

NOTES & SOURCES

The area known as Northern New Mexico is land that the Jicarilla Apache, Pueblo, Ute, and Comanche peoples have lived in relation to for uncountable years. Much of my writing happened on the opposite coast, though, on the ancestral lands of the Narragansett people, now called Providence, Rhode Island. I am also always drawing on my home in Santiago, Chile, in the valley of the Río Mapocho: Picunche land.

Recognizing the land is an expression of gratitude and a way of honoring the Indigenous people who have been living and working on this vast island of many names since time immemorial. I myself exist because of interwoven processes of colonization and resistance, violence and migration. I try to carry, or at least hold, my ancestors from the many sides of these histories in me and my writing, while affirming that the land must and will return to the people.

A NEW PATCH OF SAND

Fernald, Alexander G., Terrell T. Baker, and Steven J. Guldan. "Hydrologic, Riparian, and Agroecosystem Functions of Traditional Acequia Irrigation Systems." *Journal of Sustainable Agriculture* 30, no. 2 (2007): 147–71.

Montgomery, Molly. "The Future of Acequias: 'The Veins of Our Community.'" *Rio Grande SUN*, September 28, 2019. http://www.riograndesun.com/news/the-future-of-acequias-the-veins-of-our-community/article_757566d0-e139-11e9-ab8d-9bb55ad43e5c.html.

New Mexico Acequia Association. "Acequia Governance Handbook." Revised November 2015. https://lasacequias.org/acequia-governance/.

Nielsen, Jamie. "Pinyon-Juniper Woodlands." National Park Service. August 14, 2017. https://www.nps.gov/articles/series.htm.

Vigil, Arnold. "Acequias: Lifeblood of the Rural North." *Taos News*, July 18, 2018. https://taosnews.com/stories/acequias-lifeblood-of-the-rural-north,5048350483.

LAMY STATION CYCLE

The small town of Lamy, NM has a historic station on Amtrak's Southwest Chief—which runs from Chicago to Los Angeles—because the terrain around nearby Santa Fe made it impossible to build tracks through the state's capital city. It is my grandparents' preferred port of arrival. The station's town was named after Jean-Baptiste Lamy, the archbishop who inspired Willa Cather's novel *Death Comes for the Archbishop*—a book my mother loves so much, she won't read the final pages and let the archbishop die.

Felipe V. Ortega, MA, passed away on Saturday, February 24, 2018. My two sisters and I had the privilege of taking basic pottery classes with Felipe in July of 2014. When Felipe passed, I was in college, taking a translation class where I'd been assigned Yoshimasu Gōzō's *Alice Iris Red Horse*. The same day I received my sister's text about Felipe, I encountered Gōzō's beautiful poem, "Lamy Station." This connection across time and space felt like something Felipe would appreciate and helped open up Gōzō's poetry to me, while inspiring my own writing.

With gratitude to Forrest Gander and C.D. Wright.

Great American Stations. "Lamy, NM (LMY)." Accessed April 9, 2020. https://www.greatamericanstations.com/stations/lamy-nm-lmy/.

Nott, Robert. "Potter Known for Having 'Secret' Method of Creating Utilitarian Clay Vessels." *Santa Fe New Mexican*, April 2, 2018. https://www.santafenewmexican.com/news/local_news/potter-known-for-having-secret-method-of-creating-utilitarian-clay/article_9a27d95f-7041-59f8-8084-9e0ff4f21dfb.html.

Ortega, Felipe V. "Ceramics for the Archaeologist: An Alternative Perspective." In *Engaged Anthropology: Research Essays on North American Archaeology, Ethnobotany, and Museology*, edited by B. Sunday Eiselt and Michelle Hegmon. Ann Arbor, MI: University of Michigan/Museum of Anthropology, 2005.

———."Preparing and Caring for Your Vessel." Owl Peak Pottery Foundation. Accessed April 9, 2020. http://www.felipeortega.com/wp-content/uploads/2018/07/CaringforyourVessel.pdf.

———."The Art and Practice of Jicarilla Apache Micaceous Pottery Manufacturing." Owl Peak Pottery Foundation. Accessed April 9, 2020. http://www.felipeortega.com/wp-content/uploads/2018/07/Felipe-Art-and-Practice.pdf.

GREENTHREAD INTERLUDE

Greenthread, or as I have always known it, cota, is a small flower native to the Southwest that can be used for tea and dyeing. I understand it is called *hohosyi* or *hohoise* in Hopi and *dééh* (tea) or *ch'il ahwééh* in Diné. It is also frequently called Navajo, Hopi, or Indian tea. Its scientific name is *Thelesperma megapotamicum*.

Bruneni, Susan. "JULY: Cota: Thelesperma Megapotamicum." Santa Fe Botanical Garden. July 2012. https://santafebotanicalgarden.org/july-2012/.

Curtin, L. S. M. *Healing Herbs of the Upper Río Grande*. Sante Fe, NM: Laboratory of Anthropology, 1947.

Hawley, Rob. "Cota - A Delicious Wild Herb Tea." *The Taos News*, November 18, 2019. https://www.taosnews.com/stories/cota-a-delicious-wild-herb-tea,60682.

PANAMERICANA

The opening poem of this section is composed of phrases and quotes from Eric Rutkow's history of the Pan-American Highway, *The Longest Line on the Map*. Rutkow notes the highway "had once been the largest foreign development project attempted by the United States" and "commanded the interest of every US president from Calvin Coolidge to Richard Nixon." Yet now, it is largely unheard-of or simply ignored in the US.

The Pan-American Highway is "the longest road in the world, running the length of the Western Hemisphere from Prudhoe Bay in Alaska to Tierra del Fuego in South America." However, it is interrupted by a sixty-mile stretch right in the middle—a region of mountains, jungle, and swamp that spans the border between Colombia and Panama, known as the Darién Gap. Many pushed for the highway's completion throughout the twentieth century, but technical challenges, environmental concerns, lack of funding, and politics all ended up mired in a delicate stasis where "[i]t appears, for the moment, that the Darien Gap is safe from the road."

The Darién region is where the Spanish first landed and began colonizing the mainland American continent in 1510. "Darién" is a Hispanicization of a word in the language of the Cueva, a people who were massacred by Spanish settlers in the ongoing genocide of Native Americans. Today, the Indigenous Guna (also Cuna or Kuna) and Emberá-Wounaan (also Chocó) nations inhabit the region. Their lifeways and resistance to colonization, including the highway, have been sustained for generations.

Rutkow, Eric. *The Longest Line on the Map: The United States, the Pan-American Highway, and the Quest to Link the Americas.* New York: Scribner, 2019.

"Berlin Wall": quote by a Colombian official in 1992, cited in Pascal Girot, "The Darien Region Between Colombia and Panama: Gap or Seal?" in Lyuba Zarsky, ed. 2012. *Human Rights and the Environment: Conflicts and Norms in a Globalizing World.* Hoboken, NJ: Taylor and Francis.

"[The Darien Gap] is one of the most ecologically diverse regions in the world because it acts as a land bridge where species from both continents intermingle," from Center for Popular Legal Assistance, "Summary Report: Closing the Darien Gap: The Pan-American Highway's Last Link," March 1996, NARA, RG 406, accession number 406-05-0028, box 1, Pan-American Highway Study 4 National Archives, Washington DC..

"Mental agony" and "the shining stream of motor cars," from "The Diary of Richard Tewkesbury on His Second Trip into the Darién Region of Panama: Notes in Brief," box 1, folder 8, Richard Albert Tewkesbury Papers, RS 21/7/22, Special Collections Department, Iowa State University Library. . Richard Tewkesbury was a short, white high school mathematics teacher from North Carolina who became obsessed with traversing and surveying the Darién Gap. He managed it on his second attempt, in 1940, with extensive, life-saving assistance from Indigenous guides, primarily from the Guna people.

"Cultural extinction": quote from an assessment commissioned by the Department of Transportation in 1974, discussed in Sierra Club v. Coleman (October 17, 1975), 405 F. Supp. 56.

AMERICÓN/CHILESBIAN

Other sections of this book contain language found in various sources, including *The New York Times* and NPR, and draw inspiration from various writers and teachers including Taylor Johnson, Aaron M. Moe, Mallika Singh, Jayson P. Smith, Cole Swenson, and TC Tolbert.

Here are some coincidences:

Before ~~my~~ beginning college, I spent the summer ~~on~~ on my grandparents' farm in New Mexico. They introduced me to a poet friend:

Jamie Ross —recommended→ a class with Forrest Gander:
Latin American Death Trip —location→ Latin America:
quite interested —in→ Death:
and —→ translation (became a topic of the course):
Forrest's wife —~~poet~~→ C.D. Wright:
~~Dot~~ passed away —earlier / that same→ year (2016, January ___):
a blood clot —develops in her leg→ on a flight:
~~a flight~~
Chile —→ ~~its~~ USA:
the same —way I flew / only 2→ months later: (2016, March ___):
I began —to study→ poetry and translation (more seriously):
a year later —(2017)→ I was in a translation class:
reading —a book estates / by Forrest Gander→ Alice Iris Red Horse (by Yoshimasu Gozo):
in which —I read a / poem titled→ Lamy Station:
the train station —that growing up / we always used→ to my grandparents:
the day after —I heard→ a potter I knew:
in my grandparents' own a ~~bed~~ —→ passes away

ACKNOWLEDGMENTS

A les trabajadores, abolitionists and anarchists, feministas, perras del futuro, estudiantes en lucha, locas y queers, people of color and Black and Indigenous revolucionarixs the world over who are and have been fighting for liberation, without whom I could not be here, writing—I have learned so much from you and have so much yet to learn, thank you.

To all my mentors, thank you. Querida Eleni Sikelianos, gracias for showing me so many ways to extend the document, and for opening ideal space in which to write, again and again. Thank you to Erica Hunt, Forrest Gander, Mónica de la Torre, and dg nanouk okpik for their lessons, insights, and suggestions. To the many teachers who have touched me in ways great and small: Leticia Alvarado, Erica Durante, Marwa Helal, Jennifer Montgomery, Rick Moody, Julio Ortega, and Ada Smailbegović, thank you. Y antes aún: Cristóbal, Lore, Gail, Lihi, gracias.

Thank you to C.D. Wright, whose guiding hand I never held, but have often felt.

Deepest thanks to Renee Gladman, whose writing is a constant inspiration, challenge, and comfort, for seeing in my words what I had hoped was there.

Thank you to Mary-Kim Arnold, Sawako Nakayasu, and Raquel Salas Rivera, whose books have served as dear teachers and guides in my translanguaging and queering of documentary poetry. Your blessings on my book mean the world.

Thank you to the lovely people at Wendy's Subway for their patience and trust in my work, and especially to Corinne Butta and Rachel Valinsky, for answering my many bewildered questions about how to bring a book to life. Thank you to William Guion, the infrared tree photographer, for his beautiful portrait of my grandparent's cottonwood in "A New Patch of Sand."

Thanks to all who read these poems in their many forms of becoming and offered thoughts, in and out of classes.

My friends, peers, loves, lovers, life-companions, dancers, collaborators, comrades: Chiara Arellano, Auriane Benabou, Stella Binion, Miles Crist, Chaelee Dalton, Maya Greenhill, Imani Elizabeth Jackson, Lili Coyote Keys, Billie McKelvie, Paula Pacheco Soto, Emmett Rahn-Oakes, Anna Lu Ramsey, Oriana van Praag, Gabriel Womark, Kayli Wren, Miranda Zhen-Yao. Thank you.

Gracias Mateo Aguilera, Amalia Ramaciotti y Xabier Usabiaga, por ese primer espacio donde escribir un nombre. Thank you to Ruth Allen and Vié Lu, for your beautiful bald heads, fellow gender destroyers. Thank you to Clare Boyle, for editing with such grace. Thank you to Caroline Sprague for growing with me as I found myself in words and body. Thank you to Gwendolyn Harper for Saturday mornings writing, and for reading at any and all hours. Thank you to Meredith Morran for sharing your shapes with me. Thank you to Abram Scharf for sitting on the other couch while the world shut down and holding me to the page. Thank you to Tara Sharma for teaching me to mind and matter the metaphor. Thank you to the moonies, Julia Chang, Sajo Jefferson, Florence Li, Ana Rosa Marx, and Mena Sachdev, for fires, for fish, for getting me through. Thank you to Alex Hanesworth, pajarito precioso—my grounding, my firmament.

Y a mi querida familia. Les ancestres que nunca conocí, guiándome cada día. Mis abuelos, tíos, tías, primix in both, all, worlds. Gracias Marce por tu cariño sin fin. Leo, Tebi y Lauris, ustedes completan mi corazón. Oli y Zoe, son les mejores sisnocis que podría imaginar. Daddy-O y Mami, que me enseñaron a ver, documentar, y escribir con tanto cuidado y rigurosidad, gracias por todo.

Americón
© 2022 Nico Vela Page

All rights reserved. No part of this book may be used or reproduced without prior permission of the publisher.

Passage Series #3
First Edition, 2022
Edition of 750 copies
ISBN: 978-1-7359242-7-4
Library of Congress Control Number: 2022936288

Copy editing by Corinne Butta and Paula Pacheco Soto
Proofreading by Mayra A. Rodríguez Castro and Rachel Valinsky
Cover design and typesetting by Rissa Hochberger
Typeset in Didot and Media 77
Printed at Jelgavas Tipogrāfija, Latvia

Cover image by Miranda Zhen-Yao Van-Boswell, *All Land Has a Perfect Memory*, 2020.

Published by Wendy's Subway
379 Bushwick Avenue
Brooklyn, NY 11206
wendyssubway.com

Wendy's Subway is a non-profit reading room, writing space, and independent publisher located in Brooklyn.

The Passage Series publishes titles by emerging writers and artists whose work manifests in innovative, hybrid, and cross-genre forms that imagine new possibilities and expressions of the poetic, the political, and the social.

Americón was selected for the 2020 Wendy's Subway Book Prize judged by Renee Gladman.

The Passage Series is supported, in part, by public funds from the New York City Department of Cultural Affairs in Partnership with the City Council.